VALUES IN ACTION ®
Twenty Real Life Stories

COMPASSION

By
Kathleen J. Edgar
Susan E. Edgar
and
Joanne Mattern

Reading
CHALLENGE®

PHOTO CREDITS

www.readingchallenge.com

a division of
Learning Challenge, Inc.
569 Boylston Street
Boston, MA 02116

0404-1MV

Library of Congress Cataloging-in-Publication Data

Edgar, Kathleen J.
Compassion / by Kathy Edgar, Susan Edgar, Joanne Mattern.
p. cm. — (Values in action, twenty real life stories)
Summary: Short biographies of men and women whose lives and work embody the value of compassion.
Includes bibliographical references and index.
ISBN 1-59203-055-6 (hardcover)
1. Biography—Juvenile literature. 2. Compassion—Juvenile literature. 3. Values—Juvenile literature.
[1. Compassion. 2. Biography.] I. Edgar, Susan E. II. Mattern, Joanne, 1963- III. Title.
CT107.E335 2003   920.02—dc22
                                          2003013727

Dear Parents and Educators:

Reading Challenge® is pleased to introduce a new Literacy and Character Education program— **Values in Action® Twenty Real Life Stories.**

These twenty fascinating biographies are perfect for classroom study, homeschooling, and supplemental reading. The stories foster an appreciation of important values that form the basis of sound character education.

Each real life story comes to life with a time line and quotes. In addition, each book contains a value-discussion section, a glossary and pronunciation guide, and an index. These elements give readers the tools they need to fully appreciate the inspiring biographies within.

"Open a book . . . and the world opens to you."

The Editors
Reading Challenge

A division of Learning Challenge, Inc.
www.learningchallenge.com

Contents

Compassion in Action

How the Lives of 20 Remarkable People Illustrate the Value of Compassion

Compassion is the ability to understand and feel for people who are suffering. A compassionate person is affected by the pain of others and reaches out to help. When a friend of yours has a cold, for instance, you might take soup when you visit, or collect his or her missed assignments from school. You know what it is like to suffer from a cold, so you do what you can to help make being sick easier for your friend. You are compassionate—you understand that your friend is going through a tough time, so you make an effort to help ease that suffering.

Some of the most important people in the world achieved great things because of their compassion. Clara Barton was a nurse who tended to wounded soldiers during the Civil War. She was deeply moved by the pain and suffering that she saw those men experience. As a result, Barton started the American Red Cross—a relief organization that supplies medicine, food, and other aid to victims of war, famine, disease, and natural disasters.

Cesar Chavez was another person whose compassion led him to greatness. He was frustrated by the terrible way that he and his fellow migrant workers were being treated. That understanding inspired him to try to change things for the better. His efforts helped end some of the terrible working conditions experienced by farm workers.

Another person of great compassion was Mother Teresa. She was a Catholic nun who dedicated her life to helping others. She cared for the sick, worked for world peace, and believed that all people should be treated with kindness and love. She gave up her own pleasures and comforts in order to help people in need.

Often, when people are treated with compassion, they become compassionate, too. They learn how good it feels to be helped by others, and are inspired to do the same. All of the people in this book were led by their feelings of compassion to take action and help others. They are excellent examples of what reaching out to others can do for humankind.

Jane Addams
Social Reformer and World Peace Activist
(born 1860 • died 1935)

During the late 1800s, hundreds of thousands of immigrants from Europe and Asia came to America's shores. As the population of the U.S. increased, fewer jobs were available. Many of the newcomers were poor and homeless. Jane Addams worked to help the poor make better lives for themselves. Her compassion made her a pioneer of the social-reform movement. She urged society to change for the better.

A Social Reformer Is Born

Born on September 6, 1860, in Cedarville, Illinois, Jane was one of nine children. Her father was a state senator and a friend of President Abraham Lincoln.

Jane Addams attended private school and Women's Medical College. She was unsure what she wanted to do with her life. When she was 27, Addams traveled to Europe with her friend Ellen Starr. While in England, they visited Toynbee Hall, a settlement house in London. Settlement houses offered cultural and

Jane Addams, photographed here as a young woman, was determined to help the poor make better lives for themselves.

educational programs to poor families. They helped bring new life to communities. Addams and Starr were impressed by this idea and returned home with plans to create a settlement house in Chicago.

> "Social advance depends quite as much upon an increase in moral sensibility as it does upon a sense of duty."
>
> —Jane Addams

Hull House

First, Jane Addams and Ellen Starr rented the Hull estate, a large, run-down mansion in a poor section of Chicago. After making some repairs, the two women opened Hull House in 1889. Modeled after Toynbee Hall in London, Hull House helped needy families. It also offered educational programs for immigrants, and day care for the children of working parents.

During the next several years, 12 more buildings were added, making Hull House one of the largest centers of its kind in the United States. Private citizens and other charity groups donated funds to keep the settlement growing. Hull House also offered training programs for people who wanted jobs as social workers.

Following the success of Hull House, Addams turned her talents to social and work issues. She spoke out on topics such as public education, labor reform, and the rights of immigrants. She worked to create laws to help average people. These laws included limiting work to eight hours each day, providing wages to workers who got hurt on the job, and making sure that factories were safe.

Pleading for Peace

In 1914, World War I broke out in Europe. Addams believed that people should live peacefully and not harm each other. In 1915, she traveled to the Netherlands. There, she joined more than 1,000 women from Europe and North America to discuss putting an end to the war. Known as the International Congress of Women, the group wanted to meet with government officials from the warring nations in "protest against the madness and horror of war." Addams was elected president of the Congress.

The Congress chose 30 women to travel through Europe. As president of the group, Addams represented women who had lost loved ones in the war. The group insisted that average citizens and prisoners of war be treated fairly. They also suggested that a Society of Nations be established to act as a worldwide governing body. World War I

TOPICAL TIDBIT

The United Nations

The United Nations (UN) is an international organization dedicated to maintaining peace throughout the world. Based on a proposal drafted by the International Congress of Women in 1915, the United Nations Charter was signed by representatives from 51 nations on June 26, 1945, in San Francisco, California. (A *charter* is an official document that creates an organization and spells out its rules and regulations.)

lasted until November 1918. But government officials did adopt many of the ideas presented by the International Congress of Women—especially those regarding the treatment of prisoners of war.

After the war, Addams kept working for reform. In 1920, she helped found the American Civil Liberties Union (ACLU). It is still active today. In 1931, she was awarded the Nobel Peace Prize for her efforts in social work and pleading for peace throughout the world.

Worthy of Remembrance

Jane Addams died on May 21, 1935, in Chicago. Hull House, now a museum, remains as a monument to Addams. She was one of the greatest social reformers in U.S. history. ◇

LIFE EVENTS

1860
Jane Addams is born in Cedarville, Illinois.

1889
Addams and Ellen Starr open Hull House in Chicago.

1910
Addams's auto-biography, entitled *Twenty Years at Hull House*, is published.

1919-1935
Addams helps found, and serves as president of, the Women's International League for Peace and Freedom.

1931
Addams is awarded the Nobel Peace Prize in recognition of her efforts in social work and reform.

1935
Jane Addams dies.

Clara Barton
Founder of the American Red Cross
(born 1821 • died 1912)

Clara Barton devoted her life to helping others—on battlefields and in hospitals. She started the American Association of the Red Cross (now called the American Red Cross). It is a relief organization that continues to provide supplies, medicine, food, and funds to people who are victims of war, natural disasters, disease, and famine.

Independent Spirit

Clarissa Harlowe Barton was born on December 25, 1821, in Oxford, Massachusetts. She was schooled at home by her brothers and sisters, who were much older than she was. She gained nursing experience by caring for one of her brothers, who was ill. When she was 15, she became a teacher.

In 1852, Barton started her own school in Bordentown, New Jersey. Under her leadership, many new students came to the school. However, town officials told Barton that the school had become too big to be managed by a woman—a man

Clara Barton was called the "Angel of the Battlefield" for her compassionate work.

would have to run it. In that era, people had limited ideas about what a woman could and could not do. As a result, Barton resigned.

Before the Civil War began in 1861, Barton worked as a clerk. It was unusual for "proper" women to work outside the home, but for Barton it was more acceptable because she was not married. When the Civil War broke out, Barton left her job to help wounded Union soldiers.

> **"I may be compelled to face danger, but never fear it, and while our soldiers can stand and fight, I can stand and feed and nurse them."**
>
> —Clara Barton

Relief Agent

Barton raised money to provide relief (food and medical supplies) for the soldiers. She served as a nurse, assisting surgeons who had to remove bullets, stitch up wounds, or amputate soldiers' arms and legs. She worked endless hours to help the men, earning the nickname "Angel of the Battlefield."

After the war ended in 1865, President Abraham Lincoln gave Barton a new job: helping families find missing soldiers. Then, in 1869, Barton went to Europe to rest. While there, she learned of an organization that had been formed in Switzerland in 1864. It was called the International Red Cross.

TOPICAL TIDBIT

The International Red Cross

The idea for the International Red Cross (IRC) came from Henri Dunant, a Swiss humanitarian, who had seen wounded soldiers left to die during the Battle of Solferino, in Italy, in 1859. In 1863, delegates from 16 countries attended a meeting in Switzerland, called the Geneva Convention. They founded the IRC to help the wounded.

Barton volunteered at the International Red Cross to help soldiers wounded in the Franco-Prussian War (1870-1871). However, the organization would not let her treat war victims because she was a woman. So Barton worked independently. She returned to the United States in 1873. She urged the country to begin its own branch of the Red Cross organization.

American Association of the Red Cross

Although the Red Cross provided many important services, the U.S. government was not interested in starting such an organization. Government officials wanted to stay out of Europe's wars and problems. They considered the Red Cross to be a European organization. Barton worked long

LIFE EVENTS

1821
Clarissa Harlowe Barton is born in Oxford, Massachusetts.

1862
Barton serves as a front-line nurse for the Army of the Potomac.

1863
Barton serves as superintendent of nurses for the Army of the James. The same year, in Europe, the International Red Cross is founded.

1870
Barton serves in Europe during the Franco-Prussian War.

1881
Barton founds the American Red Cross. She serves as its president until 1904.

1912
Barton dies in Glen Echo, Maryland.

and hard to convince U.S. leaders to start the American Association of the Red Cross (now called the American Red Cross).

She finally succeeded in 1881 and opened the American branch of the Red Cross. Barton thought that Red Cross organizations should provide relief services to people during *all* times—in peace and in war. She urged the International Red Cross to adopt what is called the "American Amendment." It called for the organization to help victims of natural disasters and food shortages as well as war victims.

Barton became the head of the American branch. She directed relief activities during the Spanish-American War, in 1898. She also oversaw assistance to victims of disasters, such as the 1889 flood in Johnstown, Pennsylvania, and the 1900 hurricane that nearly wiped out Galveston, Texas.

Despite her hard work, Barton had trouble being in charge of other people. She wanted to do things herself or in her own way. Barton was asked to resign in 1904, and did. She died on April 12, 1912, in Glen Echo, Maryland.

Barton's Legacy

The American Red Cross has helped millions of people since 1881. It is a fitting tribute to the compassion of its founder, who worked selflessly to relieve the suffering of the sick, wounded, and homeless. ◇

Cesar Chavez
The Worker's Friend
(born 1927 • died 1993)

Every year, thousands of people travel around the country, harvesting crops for very low pay. For decades, these people, known as migrant workers, had little hope or a chance for a better life. Then one man stepped forward to help them find fair treatment and respect. His name was Cesar Chavez.

A Poor Childhood

Cesar Estrada Chavez was born on March 31, 1927, near Yuma, Arizona. Years before, his grandfather had come to the U.S. from Mexico, and had started a small farm. During the 1930s, the Great Depression hit. This was a time when the country fell into serious economic trouble. Cesar's family lost the farm because he could not afford to pay the taxes. The family got in their car and drove to California to start a new life.

Cesar, his five brothers and sisters, and their parents became migrant workers. They traveled all over California, picking crops for 12 hours a day, six days a week. It was a very difficult life. Migrant-worker

*Cesar Chavez's compassion made life
better for migrant workers.*

families lived in tiny shacks with no running water or bathrooms. Workers were paid very little for their hard labor. They were afraid to complain, though, because then they would lose their jobs.

Because the Chavez family had to keep moving to find work, Cesar attended more than 30 schools by the time he finished eighth grade. Teachers did not pay much attention to him. He could barely read or write. Still, he managed to learn some English, a skill that became important later in his life.

"Don't Buy Grapes!"

> "Every time you go to the store and choose not to buy grapes, you cast a vote."
> —Cesar Chavez

Cesar quit school after eighth grade and found a job picking grapes in California's vineyards. In time, he became tired of the terrible working conditions. He tried to convince the other workers to ask the vineyards' owners for more money and a better place to live. But the workers were afraid to complain.

When Cesar Chavez was in his early 20s, he met a man named Fred Ross. Ross worked for the Community Services Organization (CSO), a group trying to help migrant workers. Soon Chavez was doing volunteer work for the organization. When his farm boss found out, he thought that Chavez would cause trouble among the migrant workers, so he fired him.

Chavez then got a full-time job with the Community Services Organization. He worked hard, organizing meetings, registering workers to vote, and getting them into school. He also organized citizenship classes for Mexican workers.

In 1962, Chavez left the Community Services Organization to start his own organization, the National Farm Workers Association (NFWA). The NFWA was a huge success. Its members worked together to fight for the rights of migrant workers. The NFWA also provided other important services, such as selling goods cheaply to migrant families, lending them money, and hiring lawyers to help workers who were treated unfairly by their employers.

In 1965, the NFWA decided to take drastic action to win better pay and working conditions: They went on strike. The farm owners fought back by hiring people from Mexico to come and work for little pay. It looked as if the strike would go on for a long time.

Then Chavez came up with a plan to force the farm owners to settle. He and other NFWA members traveled all over America, asking people to boycott (refuse to buy) California grapes. They asked store owners not to sell them, truck drivers not to deliver them, and people everywhere not to buy or eat them. Chavez

TOPICAL TIDBIT

Giving Names to the Nameless

The plight of migrant farm workers first came to many Americans' attention in 1948, when a plane carrying 28 Mexicans crashed near Los Gatos, California. Songwriter Woody Guthrie was moved to compose a song, "Deportee (Plane Wreck at Los Gatos)." In it, he described the victims "all scattered like dry leaves" on the brown hills of Los Gatos Canyon. He also gave the workers names—such as Juan and Maria—to make the point that Americans didn't know about the struggles of the people who picked their food.

made many speeches and appeared in many newspapers. In time, people all over the country began to learn about the migrants' suffering. More and more people demanded fair treatment for the farm workers.

The grape boycott worked. Eventually, boycotts spread to other farm products, such as lettuce and tomatoes. In 1970, the farm owners finally agreed to make changes, and the strike ended. The farm workers had won.

Cesar Chavez continued to work with farm workers until his death on April 23, 1993. He helped end some of the worst conditions in the farm workers' existence, making life better for thousands of people. ◇

LIFE EVENTS

1927
Cesar Estrada Chavez is born near Yuma, Arizona.

1958
Chavez becomes general director of the Community Service Organization (CSO).

1962
Chavez starts the National Farm Workers Association (NFWA).

1965
The NFWA begins a historic strike against California grape farmers.

1971
The NFWA and the AFL-CIO join to form a new union—the United Farm Workers of America (UFW).

1993
Cesar Chavez dies.

Diana
Princess of Wales
(born 1961 • died 1997)

The Princess of Wales stepped out of a life of privilege to help people in need.

When Lady Diana Spencer married Great Britain's Prince Charles, millions of people worldwide watched the wedding on television. People were fascinated by the shy, beautiful woman who was now a princess. Diana was popular with the British people. She was known for her beauty, grace, and compassion. Diana's life, however, was far from a fairy tale. She struggled with depression, an eating disorder, the end of her marriage, and the intrusion of the media.

> **"I've always thought that people need to feel good about themselves, and I see my role as offering support to them, to provide some light along the way."**
>
> —Diana, Princess of Wales

A Friend of the Royals

Born July 1, 1961, in Sandringham, England, Diana Frances Spencer was the daughter of wealthy parents. The family lived on an estate that her father rented from the royal family. Diana, one of four Spencer children, knew the queen's family during her childhood. They were neighbors.

When Diana was a child, her parents divorced. It was a tough and lonely time for the little girl. Her mother left the family, and Diana and her siblings remained with their father. Diana was sent to boarding schools in England and Switzerland.

Upon her return to England, she found work as a nanny. Later, she became a kindergarten teacher. Diana loved working with children. Her great skill with them continued throughout her life.

She soon began to date Prince Charles, who was 12 years older. The couple announced their engagement on February 24, 1981. At that time, Diana was very timid around the news media—so much so that she was often referred to as "Shy Di." She was not accustomed to living a public life and having her every move photographed. Photographers loved her, however. Charmed by her beauty, shyness, and grace, they continued to pursue and photograph her.

TOPICAL TIDBIT

In Line for the Throne

Diana's sons, Prince William of Wales and Prince Harry, are almost as popular with the press as their mother was. Both are somewhat more protected from the media. However, William is especially fascinating to many people, partly because he looks very much like his mother. (His handsome face often graces teen magazine covers as a "heartthrob.") He is also just as compassionate as Diana was, devoting much of his time to charity work. "My mother used her position very well to help other people . . . and I hope to do the same," Prince William has said.

Wedding of the Century

Charles and Diana got married on July 29, 1981. Millions of people worldwide watched them exchange vows on television. Viewers were enchanted by the royal wedding and watching Diana become a princess. At first, the couple seemed very happy, especially following the birth of their first child, Prince William, in 1982. Their second son, Prince Henry (known as Harry), was born in 1984.

As Her Royal Highness, the Princess of Wales, Diana attended many public functions with her husband. She accompanied him on trips to foreign countries and became involved in many charities. At one time, she was said to be president of more than 100 organizations. Diana enjoyed reaching out to others. But royal life was demanding and she had little or no privacy.

Over time, Charles and Diana became distant from each other. They legally separated in 1992. Around that time, Diana confessed that she had suffered from depression, an eating disorder, loneliness, and low self-esteem. This surprised many people. The public had thought of her as someone with few problems. She seemed to be living a happy life as a glamorous and famous princess. But she was a person, just like everyone else. She had problems, too. In 1996, Charles and Diana were divorced.

Life After Divorce

Diana lost the title of Her Royal Highness, but continued to be a member of the royal family because she was the mother of two princes. Devoting much of her time to her sons, she wanted to step out of the spotlight. She asked the media to give her some space. She cut back on her charity work for a while.

In time, Diana went back to her charity work. She gave a lot of her time to the homeless, sufferers of AIDS, victims of land mines, and organizations devoted to helping children around the world. She surprised many people by touching, holding, and hugging children with AIDS. By doing so, she showed the world that they did not have to be afraid of people with AIDS. She taught people how to have compassion for people with serious diseases.

LIFE EVENTS

1961
Diana Frances Spencer is born in Sandringham, England.

1981
Lady Diana Spencer and Prince Charles are married at St. Paul's Cathedral in London.

1982
Charles and Diana's first son, Prince William, is born.

1984
Prince Henry (known as Harry) is born.

1980s-1990s
Diana dedicates much of her time to charity work.

1996
Diana and Charles are divorced.

1997
Diana dies in a car accident in Paris, France.

"The People's Princess"

The press had never given up chasing Diana to photograph her and report on her activities. On August 31, 1997, Diana and her friend Dodi Fayed were in Paris, France. The car they were in, which was speeding to escape from photographers, crashed. Diana, Fayed, and their driver were killed. News of Diana's death, at age 36, shocked and saddened millions of people around the world.

Princess Diana gave youth and style to Britain's royal family, which was often considered boring and stuffy. She was more than glitter and glamour, however. Despite her personal problems, Diana devoted her life to others—including her sons and the many charities she supported. Called "England's Rose" and "the people's princess," she is still mourned and missed by many people throughout the world. ◇

Thomas A. Dooley
The Jungle Doctor
(born 1927 • died 1961)

Some people become heroes because they act bravely in battle, explore dangerous places, or perform incredible feats. Another way some people become heroes is by helping others. Thomas A. Dooley was one of those heroes.

Musical Beginnings

Thomas Anthony Dooley was born in St. Louis, Missouri, on January 17, 1927. He was interested in music as a child. Thomas took piano lessons for many years and performed with orchestras in St. Louis.

Thomas's family wanted him to become a professional concert pianist. However, young Thomas Dooley had decided that a career in music was not for him. He wanted to study medicine.

In 1944, Dooley started college at the University of Notre Dame in Indiana. At that time, the U.S. was involved in World War II. Dooley decided that he owed his service to his country. He dropped out of college to serve in the U.S. Navy from 1944 until

1946. Then he went back to school. He received a Doctor of Medicine degree from St. Louis University in 1953.

> "My years in Asia have proved to me that the brotherhood of man exists as certainly as does the fatherhood of God."
>
> —Thomas A. Dooley

A Life-changing Assignment

In May 1954, the country of Vietnam, in Southeast Asia, was ending a long war with France. As part of an agreement the two countries made to stop the fighting, Vietnam was to be divided into two zones, North and South. Because North Vietnam was to be ruled by a Communist government, many Vietnamese chose to flee to the South, which had a more democratic government. Suddenly, this created many, many refugees.

Dr. Thomas A. Dooley volunteered for duty aboard the U.S.S. *Montague,* a Navy ship that transported refugees from North Vietnam to South Vietnam. The Americans called this evacuation of more than 600,000 people "the Passage to Freedom."

Dooley was horrified at the conditions that the Vietnamese refugees had to endure. They had little food, no clean water, and no medical care. As a

Dr. Thomas A. Dooley with some of his young friends at his MEDICO hospital in northern Laos.

medical officer in the city of Haiphong, Dooley's job was to prevent the spread of disease. Later, he was put in charge of building and maintaining Haiphong's refugee camps.

The Americans had to leave Haiphong in May 1955, when the Communist government took over the city. Dooley returned to the U.S. and wrote a book about his experiences in Vietnam. That book, *Deliver Us From Evil*, became a best-seller. It was translated into 11 different languages. Dooley also became the youngest U.S. Navy Medical Corps officer to receive the Navy's Legion of Merit.

Dooley traveled around the U.S. giving lectures about the Navy's work in Vietnam. However, he could not stop thinking about the refugees and the terrible conditions they endured. He knew that he had to go back to Southeast Asia and help.

Jungle Hospitals

In 1956, Dooley quit the Navy and joined the International Rescue Committee. Using some of the money he had earned from his book and lectures, he traveled to Nam Tha. This is a village in northern Laos, a country that borders Vietnam. Dooley chose Laos because he knew they needed a lot of help. The country had millions of people and few doctors.

Dooley and several of his friends started a hospital in Nam Tha. The hospital, which was located in the middle of the jungle, had no electricity, plumbing, air-conditioning, or modern medical equipment. Still, Dooley treated about 100 patients every day. He also trained local people to provide medical care, so that they could run the hospital after he left.

In November 1957, Dooley founded an organization called the Medical International Cooperation Organization, or MEDICO. MEDICO provided doctors and nurses, hospitals, and medical treatment to people in Southeast Asia.

By 1958, Tom Dooley was widely admired in the U.S. Everyone from schoolchildren to secretaries raised money and sent supply packages to MEDICO. Dooley also made many radio and television appearances to raise money.

Soon after he founded MEDICO, Tom Dooley found out that he had cancer. In August 1959, he returned to the U.S. to have a cancerous tumor

TOPICAL TIDBIT

Another Tom Dooley

By coincidence, two people named Tom Dooley were famous at the same time. In 1958, the Kingston Trio, a popular folk group, had a hit with a traditional American ballad called "Tom Dooley." The song told the true story of a man who killed a woman in 1866. The coincidence caused some confusion at the time—many people thought that the song was about the famous doctor!

removed. Despite his illness, he refused to stop working. By October, he had raised one million dollars for MEDICO; by Christmas, he was back in Laos.

In 1960, Dooley wrote *The Night They Burned the Mountain*, about the founding of MEDICO and his adventures in Southeast Asia. By June of that year, however, the cancer had spread through his body. Dooley returned to New York for treatment. He died on January 18, 1961—one day after his 34th birthday.

On June 7, 1962, President John F. Kennedy honored Dr. Thomas A. Dooley by presenting a gold medal to his mother. The President hailed the Jungle Doctor for "providing a model of American compassion before the rest of the world." ◇

LIFE EVENTS

1927
Thomas Anthony Dooley is born in St. Louis, Missouri.

1944
Dooley drops out of Notre Dame to join the Navy during World War II.

1954
Dooley volunteers to help relocate 600,000 refugees from North to South Vietnam.

1956
Deliver Us From Evil, Dooley's book about Vietnam, makes him a popular figure in the U.S.

1957
Dooley forms MEDICO to provide Southeast Asians with medical care.

1961
Thomas A. Dooley dies.

Frederick Douglass

A Voice Against Slavery

(born 1818 • died 1895)

A photo of Frederick Douglass as a young man.

Frederick Douglass endured cruel mistreatment as a slave. Later, he transformed himself into a powerful and compassionate voice for freedom.

A Slave Child

Frederick Bailey was born in a slave cabin in Easton, Maryland, in February 1818. Like many slave children, he was taken away from his

> "I am no coward. Liberty I will have, or die in the attempt to gain it."
> —Frederick Douglass

mother. Young Frederick was raised by his grandparents, who were also slaves.

When Frederick was six years old, his grandmother took him to the plantation where his master lived. Frederick had to do hard work for long hours. If he did not do what he was told, he was beaten. He had little food, and had to sleep on a dirt floor with only an old flour sack for a blanket.

Things got better for Frederick when he was eight years old. He was sent to Baltimore, Maryland, to live with a man named Hugh Auld. There, he did household chores and ran errands for the Auld family. In this new household, Frederick had good food to eat and warm clothes to wear. He was allowed to play with the Aulds' young son, Thomas. Mrs. Auld began teaching Frederick how to read.

It was, however, strictly against the law to teach a black person to read or write. When Mr. Auld found out what his wife was doing, he demanded that she stop her lessons. But young Frederick still wanted to learn. He convinced some of the white children in the neighborhood to share their books with him. His curious mind soaked up everything.

When Frederick was a teenager, Mr. Auld died. Frederick was sent to work on a farm. Once again, he was given little food and had to live under harsh conditions. He was often whipped when he refused to obey his master. No matter what happened to him, though, no punishment could break Frederick Bailey's spirit.

A New Life

Frederick Bailey was determined to find a way to get to the North, where slavery was illegal. Luckily, he had a friend who was a free black man. This man was willing to lend Frederick his identification papers. In 1838, using the friend's papers, 20-year-old Frederick took a train and made it all the way to New York City. He was free! He soon settled in New Bedford, Massachusetts, and changed his name to Frederick Douglass.

Although he was finally free, life was still hard. Because he was black, Douglass had trouble finding work. Finally, he got a job loading cargo onto ships.

While living in New Bedford, Douglass began attending meetings of abolitionists, people who were united in the cause of ending slavery. In 1841, Douglass spoke before the Massachusetts Anti-Slavery Society. The audience was spellbound by his stories of life as a slave. The Society asked Douglass to travel around New England, speaking about the evils of slavery.

Audiences rushed to his speeches—but not everyone was there to listen to his message. Douglass was often laughed at and attacked by mobs of angry whites. However, just as he had during his slave days, Douglass refused to back down.

Douglass later wrote a book about his life, *Narrative of the Life of Frederick Douglass, an American Slave*. It made him famous all over the world. However, this fame was dangerous. Douglass was a runaway slave, which meant that—by law—he could be captured and sent back to his master at any time.

For his own safety, Douglass went to live in England for a time. After two years, he returned home and bought his freedom from his old master. The cost was $710.96.

Freedom for Everyone

In 1847, Douglass and his family moved to Rochester, New York. The Douglass house became a stop on the Underground Railroad, which was a secret network that helped runaway slaves reach freedom in Canada. Douglass started an abolitionist newspaper called *The North Star*, which was praised by other abolitionists. His passionate writing and public speaking made him a leader in the antislavery movement. White people everywhere were surprised to learn that a black man, an ex-slave, could be so smart.

During the Civil War, Douglass became a trusted friend and adviser to President Abraham Lincoln. Douglass urged Lincoln to allow former slaves to fight for the North. He also helped win better pay and better treatment for black soldiers.

In 1865, the Thirteenth Amendment to the Constitution finally outlawed slavery in the U.S. After the end of slavery, Douglass spoke out against segregation—the practice of keeping blacks and whites separated in public places. Douglass was also the first African American to

TOPICAL TIDBIT

Words of Freedom

By 1848, Frederick Douglass had come a long way. A famous writer with a family, a home, and a busy, important life, he did something that few ex-slaves could ever do: He wrote a letter to his ex-master. "I am your fellow-man, but not your slave," Douglass said in the letter, which was published in the press and read by many Americans.

hold important positions in the U.S. government, including U.S. marshal and U.S. minister to Haiti.

Frederick Douglass was a compassionate man who believed in equal rights for everyone, not just blacks. He was active in the women's suffrage movement, which fought to win the right for women to vote. Douglass died on February 20, 1895. His belief that anyone—black or white, woman or man—could change society is an example that still inspires us today. ◇

LIFE EVENTS

1818
Frederick Bailey is born.

1838
Bailey escapes north to freedom and changes his last name to Douglass.

1841
Douglass becomes a popular speaker and a leader of the abolitionist movement.

1845
The Life and Times of Frederick Douglass is published. In 1847, Douglass starts an antislavery publication, *The North Star.*

1861
Douglass is made special adviser to President Lincoln. After the Civil War, he becomes the first black citizen to hold high rank in the U.S. government. He dies in 1895.

Varian Fry
A Forgotten Hero
(born 1907 • died 1967)

Many heroes are honored and celebrated by people all over the world. Others do their work quietly and receive little recognition. Varian Fry was one of those quiet, compassionate heroes. His efforts saved thousands of lives during World War II, but few people ever knew his name.

A Lonely Childhood

Varian Mackey Fry was born in New York City on October 15, 1907. He grew up in nearby Ridgewood, New Jersey. He was an only child, and was often lonely. Classmates teased Varian because his first name sounded like a girl's, he wore glasses, and was not very good at sports. All these things kept him from fitting in with his classmates.

When Varian was a teenager, he attended an all-boys school in New England. Although he did well in school, Varian was horrified at the hazing, or tormenting, of underclassmen by the seniors. During his third year, he was told to cross a room by hanging hand over hand from a hot steam pipe.

The writer Varian Fry dropped everything in his quiet New York life to help rescue refugees in Nazi-occupied France.

Varian refused, then went to the school's headmaster. He said that he was so opposed to the school's hazing traditions, he no longer wished to attend the school. The next day, his father took him home. Varian attended another school, then went on to Harvard University. After graduating from Harvard, he worked as a magazine writer in New York.

Working in Secret

In 1939, World War II broke out in Europe. In 1940, the German army invaded and occupied France. French Jews and other citizens were being sent to concentration camps, where thousands were killed. Shortly after the German occupation began, Fry went to Marseilles, France, as a representative of a private U.S. relief committee. Besides the regular work he did for that organization, Fry often worked behind the scenes, doing many illegal things to help French refugees escape from the Nazis.

> "In all, we saved some two thousand human beings. We ought to have saved many times that number. But we did what we could."
>
> —Varian Fry

Fry set up a secret network to rescue people who were in danger from the Nazis. He faked signatures on documents in order to get work permits that French citizens could use to escape to the U.S. Fry helped more than 2,000 people in this way. Some of the people he helped were famous, such as artist Marc Chagall; others were ordinary citizens. All of them were grateful to Fry for the important work he was doing.

When the U.S. government found out what Fry was doing, it ordered him to return home. Fry refused to go, however, and continued his work.

Fry no longer had a passport or legal right to stay in France. This made his work there even more dangerous. He was watched and often questioned by French authorities, who were under Nazi control. Fry later said, "I stayed because the refugees needed me. But it took courage, and courage is a quality that I hadn't previously been sure I possessed."

Finally, in September 1941, the French government forced Fry to leave the country. He was considered an "undesirable alien" who helped Jews and opposed the Nazis.

TOPICAL TIDBIT

Saved From the Nazis

The list of refugees Varian Fry helped rescue from the Nazis includes many famous names. The painter Marc Chagall and the writer Hannah Arendt are among them. Many other noted artists, writers, and scientists who later became U.S. citizens also fled from the Nazis during those years, including Igor Stravinsky, a famous composer, and Thomas Mann, a famous novelist.

Punished for Good Deeds

After leaving France, Fry returned home to New York. He wanted to tell Americans about the terrible things the Nazis were doing to the Jews in Europe. He wrote an article for *The New Republic* magazine, entitled "The Massacre of the Jews." It was published in December 1942. Later, he wrote a book, called *Surrender on Demand*, about his experiences in France.

Instead of listening to Fry's information, however, U.S. officials became suspicious of him. They considered him a dangerous troublemaker. The Federal Bureau of Investigation (FBI) opened a file on Fry and kept him under observation for many years.

Varian Fry spent the rest of his life writing and editing books and magazines on foreign affairs. He also wrote for businesses and taught classical literature. He died suddenly in his sleep on September 13, 1967. He was 59 years old.

> "We owe Varian Fry a promise . . . never to forget the horror that he struggled against so heroically, [and] to do whatever is necessary to ensure that such horrors never happen again."
>
> —Warren Christopher, U.S. Secretary of State, on February 2, 1996

Shortly before Fry's death, the French government realized how much good work he had done. It presented him with one of its highest awards, the Legion of Honor, for his work in Marseilles. In 1991, the U.S. finally honored Varian Fry by awarding him the Eisenhower Liberation Medal. In 1993-1994, his work was the subject of an exhibition at the United States Holocaust Memorial Museum in Washington, D.C. Varian Fry also was honored as a Commemorative Citizen of the State of Israel in 1998, more than 30 years after his death. It was a fitting tribute to a compassionate man who dedicated his own life to saving the lives of others. ◇

LIFE EVENTS

1907
Varian Mackey Fry is born in New York City.

1940
The German army occupies France at the start of World War II. Fry volunteers for the Emergency Rescue Committee.

1942
"The Massacre of the Jews," an article written by Fry, is an early warning of the Holocaust.

1945
Fry's memoirs, *Surrender on Demand*, are published.

1967
Varian Fry dies.

1991
Varian Fry receives his first official recognition from the U.S. government.

Jane Goodall
Ethologist
(born 1934)

Jane Goodall lived in the jungles of Africa to study chimpanzees in their natural habitat. When she first began to study the chimps' behavior, she hid behind trees and lay on the ground so as not to frighten them. Eventually, she won their trust and observed them more closely than any human had before. For more than 40 years, she has devoted her career to studying chimpanzees. Her books, reports, and TV specials have changed the way the world looks at these incredible animals.

Early Love of Animals

Jane Goodall was born on April 3, 1934, in London, England. As a child, she loved animals and was curious to learn more about how they lived, what they ate, and how they behaved.

At the age of four, Jane wanted to discover how hens laid eggs. So she sat in a chicken coop for hours, as still as could be, until she finally saw a hen lay an egg. Jane's curiosity and patience would pay off again and again in her life.

When Jane was five, World War II began. The Nazis tried to take over Europe. The German air force frequently bombed England, endangering the lives of British citizens. It was a very frightening time. Young Jane often escaped thoughts of war by reading stories like *Dr. Doolittle*, about a scientist who could talk to animals. She dreamed that someday she, too, would be able to talk to animals.

> "If only we can overcome cruelty, to human and animal, with love and compassion, we shall stand at the threshold of a new era."
>
> —Jane Goodall

Jane Goodall loves the chimpanzees that she studies.

Pursuing Her Dream in Africa

When Goodall was in her early 20s, she traveled to Kenya to visit a friend. While there in 1957, she heard about scientists Louis and Mary Leakey. They were nearby, studying fossils of early humans. Goodall made an appointment to see them and immediately impressed Louis Leakey. He hired her as an assistant, and Goodall's stay in Africa continued.

Goodall enjoyed working with the Leakeys, but she was less interested in studying animals that were long dead. She was eager to study the present, the living. When Louis had the idea to study chimpanzees near Lake Tanganyika in the country now known as Tanzania, Goodall jumped at the chance.

Goodall was excited about the project, but she needed someone to go with her. Authorities in Kenya did not want a young woman to head into the wild

TOPICAL TIDBIT

Roots and Shoots

Jane Goodall has always wanted to get young people involved in environmental and animal-rights issues. In 1991, Goodall started Roots and Shoots in Dar es Salaam, Tanzania. She met with students from local schools and discussed the negative impact of hunting on animals, the environment, and even people. These students then established the same kind of discussion groups in their schools and communities. Today, there are more than 6,000 Roots and Shoots groups in more than 85 countries worldwide.

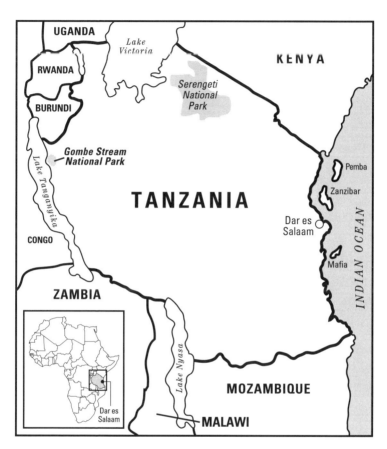

Jane Goodall has spent many years in Tanzania—at Gombe Stream National Park and in the capital, Dar es Salaam.

alone. The camp where the study would be set up was isolated and rustic. When Goodall's mother, Vanne, volunteered to accompany her, Goodall was allowed to go. They set out for Gombe Stream Game Reserve (now Gombe Stream National Park) in 1960.

Becoming a Chimp Expert

Jane Goodall's stay in Tanzania was supposed to last only three months, but it lasted much longer. Her first months there were spent watching the chimps through binoculars. If she got too close, the chimps would run away. Slowly, however, they got used to her presence and allowed her to observe their private lives.

By getting so close, Goodall saw things that no human had ever seen before. She learned, firsthand, that many ideas that people had about chimpanzees were false. For example, she watched chimps hunt other animals for food. Until then, people thought that chimps were strict vegetarians.

Goodall also saw chimps make tools out of sticks and use them. Previously, experts had believed that only humans were capable of using tools. Goodall watched as chimps put the sticks into termite or ant nests for the insects to crawl onto, then pull out the sticks and eat the insects. Goodall was fascinated.

In some ways, Goodall approached her work differently from other scientists. For instance, she gave each chimp a name, such as Gremlin or Galahad. Most scientists assigned numbers to their subjects. But Goodall was compassionate toward the animals that she studied. Giving them names, rather than numbers, meant that she respected them as fellow living beings.

Goodall published her findings in books and articles. She has become a world-renowned expert on chimps. She also earned her doctorate in ethology (the study of animals in their natural habitat).

Educating the World

Jane Goodall continues to work with chimpanzees. Her work has been the subject of many articles and *National Geographic* television specials. She founded the Jane Goodall Institute for Wildlife Research, Education, and Conservation in 1977. She continues to educate the world about chimps and important environmental issues. In 2003, she received the Global Environmental Citizen Award, which is given by the Harvard Medical School Center for Health and the Global Environment. ◇

LIFE EVENTS

1934
Jane Goodall is born in London, England.

1960
Goodall begins studying chimpanzees in Tanzania.

1965
Goodall earns her PhD in ethology at Cambridge University.

1971
Goodall publishes her first book about her work with chimpanzees, titled *In the Shadow of Man*.

1977
Goodall founds the Jane Goodall Institute for Wildlife Research, Education, and Conservation.

1988
Goodall earns the National Geographic Society Centennial Award.

Woody Guthrie
The Voice of America
(born 1912 • died 1967)

No one captured the lives of ordinary Americans in song the way Woody Guthrie did. During the middle of the 20th century, he traveled all over the U.S., writing compassionate songs that expressed the country's hopes and dreams.

A Sad Childhood

Woodrow Wilson Guthrie was born on July 14, 1912, in the small town of Okemah, Oklahoma. When he was just six years old, his older sister died in a fire. Woody's mother, Nora Guthrie, could not cope with her child's death. She also suffered from Huntington's chorea, a disease that affects the nervous system. Eventually, she had to be confined to a mental hospital.

The family also had financial problems. Woody's father, Charles Guthrie, had once had a successful business selling land. But that business began to fail. The family had to move into a run-down, abandoned house.

As a child, Woody enjoyed music. In time, Woody taught himself how to play the guitar and the harmonica. He also enjoyed watching people and finding out the stories of their lives. He was especially interested in hearing the stories of the migrant workers and drifters who passed through Okemah.

On the Road

With his mother in the hospital and his father in failing health, Woody was on his own by the age of 15. At first, he made a little money singing and playing harmonica on the streets. A few years later, he packed up his few belongings and headed to Texas. There, Woody made music with a few friends and worked at odd jobs to get by.

However, work was hard to find during the 1930s. The Great Depression had hit the country hard, and few jobs were available. To make matters worse, a severe lack of rain and poor farming methods had turned the Great Plains into a Dust Bowl. Huge dust storms filled the air, and farmers found it impossible to grow enough crops to survive.

By 1937, Woody Guthrie had traveled to California, along with thousands of other refugees from the Dust Bowl. He began to write folk songs about the workers and drifters, and about the people who had escaped to California in search of a better life. Soon, he was performing on radio stations in California and Mexico.

TOPICAL TIDBIT

The Dust Bowl

The area known as the Dust Bowl of the Great Plains extended over large parts of Colorado, Kansas, Texas, Oklahoma, and New Mexico. The dust storms that plagued the region were terrifying. High winds lifted dried-up topsoil into "black blizzards" that filled the air and blocked out the sun. People went down into basements to wait out the storms. During these long days, many people thought that the world was coming to an end.

Guthrie did not like to stay in one place for long. By 1939, he was in New York City, where he became popular among a group of musicians, writers, and artists who lived there. Guthrie also became involved in politics. He spoke out often against the unfair treatment of workers and poor people. He wrote songs very quickly, commenting on events of the day. Guthrie's most famous song, "This Land Is Your Land," said to

> "I hate a song that makes you think that you are not any good . . . that you are just born to lose. . . . I am out to fight those songs to my very last breath of air."
> —Woody Guthrie

his audiences that America belonged to them, too. It was not just for wealthy people who owned the land and the banks.

In 1943, Guthrie published his autobiography, *Bound for Glory*, which told the story of his Dust Bowl years. The book was very successful. By then, Guthrie was considered to be one of the most important folk singers in America.

For many years, Guthrie traveled around the country, singing and performing. He loved to be on the road, meeting people and telling their stories.

In the end, the thing that stopped Woody Guthrie was illness. Beginning in the late 1940s, he began having symptoms of a puzzling disability. In time, it was found to be Huntington's chorea, the same disease his mother had suffered from for so many years. Guthrie spent the last 13 years of his life in and out of hospitals as the disease gradually robbed him of his balance, speech, and ability to think clearly.

Woody Guthrie died of Huntington's chorea on October 3, 1967. But his music and his spirit live on. He has been inducted in the Songwriters' Hall of Fame and the Rock and Roll Hall of Fame, and has won many awards. Many of today's rock and country stars hail him as an inspiration, and schoolchildren all over America still sing "This Land Is Your Land." Guthrie's vivid and compassionate songs truly capture the spirit of America. ◇

LIFE EVENTS

1912
Woodrow Wilson Guthrie is born in Okemah, Oklahoma.

1937
Guthrie joins the mass migration of Dust Bowl refugees who head west to California.

1939
After achieving success on the radio in California, Guthrie leaves for New York, where he becomes part of a thriving music scene.

1943
Bound for Glory, Guthrie's auto-biography, is published.

1954
Guthrie first admits himself into Greystone Hospital in New Jersey. He is diagnosed with Huntington's chorea and dies in 1967.

Mother Jones
(Mary Harris Jones)
Mother of the
Working Class
(born 1830 • died 1930)

During the 1800s and 1900s, workers all over the U.S. fought bitter battles to win their rights and improve working conditions. One of the greatest heroes of this battle was Mary Harris Jones—a woman who looked like a sweet little grandmother. In truth, this "grandmother" was a strong speaker and an inspiration to workers everywhere. They called her Mother Jones.

A Family Tradition

Mary Harris was born in Cork, Ireland, on May 1, 1830. Her family had a tradition of fighting for their rights against the British. Her grandfather had been an Irish freedom fighter, and he was hanged for his activities. In 1835, Mary's father was forced to flee from Ireland and take his family to Canada.

Mother Jones spoke out for laborers' rights.

Mary grew up in Toronto, Ontario. After she graduated from high school, she moved to the U.S. to find work. She taught school in Michigan, but did not like "bossing little children." So she quit her job and moved to Chicago to become a dressmaker. In 1861, she married George E.

> "If they want to hang me, let them. And on the scaffold I will shout 'Freedom for the working class!'"
>
> —Mother Jones

Jones, an ironworker. Jones was a member of a labor union. He talked with his wife about the unfair struggles that workers had to go through every day at their jobs.

Starting Over

By 1867, Mary Jones was living a happy, quiet life with her husband and their four children. Then the family fell ill with yellow fever. Within a week, her husband and all her children had died of the disease.

Jones left Chicago for a time, then returned and resumed her career as a dressmaker. But in 1871, disaster struck again when the Great Chicago Fire roared through the city. Jones lost everything she owned. Once again, she was forced to start a new life.

Everyone's Mother

Jones became involved in the labor movement. She joined a group called the Knights of Labor. Soon, she was dedicating her life to the workers and their struggle for a decent life. Jones traveled from city to city to meet with workers. She lived with them in tent colonies or rundown apartments. When someone asked her where she lived, she answered, "Wherever there is a fight." Because she had no family of her own, the workers became her family. In turn, they began calling her "Mother." In time, her compassion earned her a nickname across the country—Mother Jones.

Mother Jones was especially interested in the difficult working conditions of coal miners. She attended her first United Mine Workers (UMW) convention in 1901 and worked for the organization until 1922. Her efforts to improve life for the miners earned her a new nickname: "the miners' angel."

Mother Jones had a gift for attracting attention from the press, the public, and the government. In 1902, she led a march of miners' wives into the Pennsylvania coalfields. There, the women used brooms and mops to chase away strikebreakers. In 1903, she led a "children's crusade" of several hundred workers from the textile mills of

Pennsylvania to President Theodore Roosevelt's home in New York—a journey, on foot, of 100 miles. Her march brought attention to the evils of child labor and helped end the practice of sending very young children to work at dangerous jobs.

Mother Jones faced many difficulties in her work, but refused to back down. She was arrested after a protest in West Virginia in 1913, when she was 83 years old. Striking mine workers and mine guards had exchanged gunfire, and people were killed. In an effort to discourage her cause, the authorities charged Mother Jones with conspiring to commit murder. She was convicted and sentenced to 20 years in prison. Her trial captured the

TOPICAL TIDBIT

The Children's Crusade

The "children's crusade," a protest of 1903, was inspired by the plight of America's textile workers. At the time, much of the work done in textile mills was done by children. They worked 60 hours a week. It was dangerous work: Many children were missing fingers that had been torn off by machines. The Secret Service managed to keep most of the children's crusade marchers away from the mansion of President Theodore Roosevelt—but not all. Mother Jones dressed three of the boys in better clothes, slipped onto a train with them, and showed up at the President's door!

public's interest and led to a U.S. Senate investigation of conditions in the West Virginia coal mines. Meanwhile, the governor of West Virginia decided to set Mother Jones free.

Mary Harris Jones continued to travel around the country until 1926, when she was 96 years old. She organized strikes, gave speeches, and did whatever she could to help the cause that she believed in so strongly.

She died in Silver Spring, Maryland, on November 30, 1930. She was 100 years old. Mother Jones is buried in the Union Miners Cemetery in southern Illinois—among the coal miners she always called her family. ◇

LIFE EVENTS

1830
Mary Harris is born in Cork, Ireland.

1867
Now Mary Jones of Chicago, she loses her husband and children in a yellow fever epidemic.

1871
Jones loses everything in the Great Fire and becomes involved with the Knights of Labor.

1901
Known as Mother Jones, she becomes an organizer for the United Mine Workers.

1913
Jones is arrested during a miner's strike in West Virginia.

1921
Jones is invited to the Pan-American Federation of Labor in Mexico. She dies in 1930, at age 100.

Thurgood Marshall
Mr. Civil Rights
(born 1908 • died 1993)

As a lawyer, Thurgood Marshall worked tirelessly for civil rights. As the first black justice of the U.S. Supreme Court, he challenged inequality and helped bring fair treatment to people of all races.

Not Afraid to Fight

Thurgood Marshall was born on July 2, 1908, in Baltimore, Maryland. He was named for his grandfather, Thoroughgood. Young Thurgood's parents knew that education was important. They wanted his older brother to be a doctor, and decided that Thurgood would be a dentist.

Thurgood's father loved to debate. He taught his son how to fight with words—and made sure that Thurgood could back up every argument with facts. He also taught the boy not to back down from trouble. If anyone ever insulted him because of the color of his skin, Thurgood had orders to fight back.

Thurgood Marshall, wearing his judicial robe, appears during his first day at work as Associate Justice of the U.S. Supreme Court.

Thurgood often got into trouble at school for not paying attention in class. As punishment, he had to stay after school and learn part of the U.S. Constitution. He soon memorized most of that important document, which is the basis for the country's laws.

> **"Our whole constitutional heritage rebels at the thought of giving government the power to control men's minds."**
>
> —Thurgood Marshall

Separate and Unequal

By the time Marshall was attending Lincoln University, an all-black college in Pennsylvania, he knew that he didn't want to be a dentist. He had decided to become a lawyer. After college, he wanted to go to law school at the University of Maryland. However, only white students could go there. Instead, Marshall attended Howard University, a well-known black school in Washington, D.C. He graduated at the top of his class in 1933. Then he went home to Baltimore and opened a law office.

Two years later, Marshall represented a young black man named Donald Murray. Murray wanted to go to law school at the University of Maryland— the same school that had turned Marshall away. At the trial, Marshall argued that the U.S. Constitution said that Murray had a right to attend whichever school he wanted. The judges agreed, and Marshall won his case. He was so happy, he danced outside the courtroom.

In 1940, Marshall became head of the legal and education division of the National Association for the Advancement of Colored People (NAACP). The NAACP is an organization that works toward fair treatment for all Americans. Marshall's work with the NAACP gave him a new nickname: "Mr. Civil Rights."

Many of Marshall's legal battles were aimed at ending school segregation—the practice of requiring children of different races to attend separate schools. At the time, the law said that states could segregate as long as facilities for blacks were "equal" to those for whites. "Separate but equal" was the accepted idea. Time after time, however, Marshall was able to prove in court that public schools for blacks and white were

TOPICAL TIDBIT

Charles Hamilton Houston

The Supreme Court decision that created the "separate but equal" rule was *Plessy* v. *Ferguson* (1896). Charles Hamilton Houston (1895-1950), an African American who was the grandson of slaves, dedicated his life to fighting this decision. Even before Thurgood Marshall, Houston was one of the most important lawyers of the 20th century. His efforts helped lay the path for victories he would not live to see. "We were just carrying his bags, that's all," Thurgood Marshall said after winning the *Brown* v. *the Board of Education* case.

not equal. Black schools were given less money; they had fewer, older books and supplies; and were unequal in other ways as well.

In 1952, Thurgood Marshall went before the U.S. Supreme Court to argue the most important case of his career. The name of the case was *Brown* v. *the Board of Education of Topeka, Kansas*.

A black girl named Linda Brown wanted to go to a white school in her neighborhood in Topeka, Kansas. It was closer to her home, and it was a better school. Marshall argued that she had every right to attend the white school, because segregation was against the Constitution. On May 17, 1954, the U.S. Supreme Court justices agreed. The Court ruled that school segregation was wrong and illegal.

The Court's decision dealt with schools, but it had a

LIFE EVENTS

1908
Thurgood Marshall is born in Baltimore, Maryland.

1933
Marshall graduates from Howard University School of Law.

1940
Marshall wins the first of 29 cases before the U.S. Supreme Court.

1954
Marshall wins the historic case of *Brown* v. *Board of Education* before the Supreme Court.

1967
President Lyndon Johnson nominates Marshall to the Supreme Court. He serves until 1991 and dies in 1993.

far-reaching effect. The ruling that "Separate is not equal" in schools gave new power to the civil-rights movement. It was used to knock down other unequal treatment by race—in public transportation, stores and restaurants, jobs, housing, and many other areas.

The Highest Court in the Land

During the 1960s, Marshall served on the U.S. Court of Appeals and as Solicitor (lawyer) General of the United States. He used these positions to make sure that civil-rights laws were obeyed.

In 1967, President Lyndon Johnson appointed Marshall to the Supreme Court. Thurgood Marshall was the first African American to serve on the Court. Johnson said, "I believe it is the right thing to do, the right time to do it, the right man, and the right place." Marshall held the post for 24 years. During that time, he worked to win equal treatment for all Americans.

Poor health forced Marshall to retire in 1991. He died two years later, on January 24, 1993. Thousands of people paid their respects as his body lay in state in Washington, D.C. They were honoring a compassionate man who had changed the lives of millions of Americans—for the better. ◇

Florence Nightingale
Founder of Modern Nursing
(born 1820 • died 1910)

If Florence Nightingale had followed her parents' wishes, she would have married a wealthy man instead of becoming a nurse. That would not have satisfied Florence Nightingale, however. She studied nursing and put her skills to use during the Crimean War (1853-1856). Although she tended to sick and wounded soldiers for only two years during that war, she became famous throughout the world for saving lives. She is known as the founder of modern nursing.

Different Ideas

Florence Nightingale was born in Florence, Italy, on May 12, 1820. Her parents, Frances and William Edward Nightingale, were a wealthy British couple. Florence and her older sister, Parthenope, were raised in England and schooled at home by their father. Florence enjoyed her studies, particularly math.

Soldiers called Florence Nightingale the "Lady of the Lamp."

> **"I think one's feelings waste themselves in words; they ought all to be distilled into actions and into actions which bring results."**
>
> —Florence Nightingale

However, in the early 1800s, girls were supposed to be interested in subjects that prepared them to be good wives and mothers, such as cooking and sewing. Math was for boys.

But Florence was different. She wanted to become a nurse, but her parents did not approve. In those days, nursing was not a job for wealthy, educated women like Florence Nightingale. It was a job for working-class people, without much education.

That did not matter to Nightingale. She studied on her own and learned what she could about hospitals. Finally, her parents allowed her to go to nursing school. Her studies lasted only a few months—not like today's training. Nightingale believed that God had called her to help the sick and poor. She began caring for ill women in London in 1853.

Nightingale Helps the Wounded

In March 1854, England joined France and Turkey in a war against Russia. The fighting took place in Crimea (now Ukraine), so the conflict was called the Crimean War. It began when Russia invaded Turkish lands.

Wounded British soldiers were taken to Turkey for medical care. Many injured soldiers were surviving their injuries, but dying from infections and disease. In the 1850s, doctors did not know about germs. They did not realize that they could save lives by simply keeping the soldiers and their surroundings clean.

However, some health-care professionals, including Florence Nightingale, had noticed the importance of cleanliness. Although they did not yet understand why it worked, they realized that patients did better in clean conditions.

A war reporter sent news of the dying soldiers to British newspapers. People were alarmed. Nightingale wanted to help. She was appointed by Sidney Herbert, British Secretary of War, to take a team of female nurses to Turkey.

TOPICAL TIDBIT

Medical History

Doctors were only beginning to learn about germs around the time of the American Civil War (1861-1865). They did not realize the importance of sterilizing (cleaning thoroughly) their instruments after performing operations. If a soldier's wound showed signs of infection, they thought it was just part of the healing process.

Nightingale and 38 nurses arrived at the military hospital in Turkey in November. They were shocked to find no supplies, no latrines (toilets), and little food. However, there were plenty of rats and bugs. Injured soldiers were lying on straw beds on dirty floors.

At first, the male doctors refused the nurses' help. After ten days, however, more wounded arrived and the nurses were put to work. They scrubbed floors, washed clothes, cooked meals, and insisted that latrines be built and kept clean. The nurses greatly improved conditions and saved many lives. Nightingale checked on the soldiers in the evenings, carrying a lamp to guide her way. The soldiers, thankful for her help and compassion, called her the "Lady of the Lamp."

The Hero Comes Home

In 1856, Florence Nightingale returned to England to find that she was a hero. The press had told the world about her success in saving lives. However, she was not feeling well and did not like to be in the public eye. She had an unknown illness and became too sick to leave the house.

Although ill for the rest of her life, Nightingale continued to improve medical practices. With donated funds, she set up the Nightingale Training School for Nurses at St. Thomas's Hospital in

1860. She wrote letters urging the government to improve hospital care.

Lady of the Lamp Shines On

Florence Nightingale was given many awards during her lifetime, including the Royal Red Cross from Queen Victoria of England in 1883. In 1907, the king of England, Edward VII, gave her the Order of Merit. Nightingale was the first woman to receive that honor.

Florence Nightingale died on August 13, 1910, in London. She continues to be a compassionate role model to young women who want to become nurses. Her work has had a lasting impact throughout the world. ◇

LIFE EVENTS

1820
Florence Nightingale is born in Florence, Italy.

1853
Nightingale becomes a nurse in London.

1854
Nightingale and 38 nurses save lives in Turkey by keeping the hospitals and soldiers clean.

1856
Nightingale returns to England a hero.

1883
Queen Victoria honors Nightingale with the Royal Red Cross.

1907
Nightingale becomes the first woman to receive the Order of Merit, from King Edward VII.

1910
Florence Nightingale dies.

Eva Perón
Political Leader, Social Reformer, First Lady of Argentina
(born 1919 • died 1952)

As the wife of Argentine President Juan Perón *(pay-RONE)*, Eva Perón rose to the top of Argentina's government. She was a powerful and influential leader, even though the government never officially recognized her as one. Eva led social reforms that improved the quality of life for poor and working-class people.

Humble Beginnings

On May 7, 1919, María Eva Duarte was born in Los Toldos, Argentina, to Juana Ibaguren and Juan Duarte. Eva started school when she was eight. She spent her childhood raising silkworms, collecting photographs of movie stars, and performing at make-believe circuses created by her brother and sisters.

Eva Perón (right) *at a Paris reception in 1947. She sits with Argentina's ambassador, Julie Victoria Roca.*

At 15, Eva wanted to be an actor. Her mother thought that Eva was too young for an acting career, but realized that there was no stopping her. Eva was too headstrong. Mother and daughter boarded the train for Buenos Aires.

Eva's mother soon returned home. Eva stayed in Buenos Aires with family friends. Eva toured with acting troupes and landed a starring role on a radio show. Called *Biographies of Illustrious Women*, the show detailed the lives of famous women in history, such as Queen Elizabeth I, Isadora Duncan, and Catherine the Great.

> "I demanded more rights for women because I know what women had to put up with."
> —Eva Perón

A New Argentina

The 1940s were a time of political unrest in Argentina. Dictators had been in power for years, and the people of Argentina were ready for a change. They found hope in the form of Colonel Juan Domingo Perón, a man who believed in the rights of the working class. He called *descamisados*, meaning "shirtless ones" or laborers.

Eva Duarte met Juan Perón in 1944, while attending a charity benefit. They fell in love and were married on October 22, 1945. Eva and Juan Perón shared the same beliefs regarding social reforms needed in Argentina. They worked together to unite the *descamisados* into a major political force. In 1945, the laborers chose Juan Perón as their presidential candidate. In 1946, he was elected president of Argentina.

Evita!

Evita, as Eva was called by the Argentine people, kept Juan informed of the needs of average citizens. She created the Eva Perón Foundation to help the poor find housing, medical treatment, and jobs. Evita was loved by the working-class because she was compassionate about their needs. The upper class, however, disliked her. They believed that she used her power to force them to donate money to

TOPICAL TIDBIT

The Eva Perón Hospital Train

Medical supplies were in short supply in some areas of Argentina. The Eva Perón Foundation sent a "hospital train" into those areas. The special train carried medical services, doctors, and nurses to the people who needed them.

her foundation. Regardless, the Eva Perón Foundation opened hospitals and schools, built houses for the poor, provided clothes and toys for children, and granted financial aid to senior citizens.

Evita worked to earn Argentine women the right to vote in 1947. In 1952, when Juan was reelected, women entered government service for the first time.

In 1951, Evita was chosen by the people to be Juan's vice president, but military leaders would not allow it. Also, at that time, Evita learned that she had cancer. She declined the nomination in a public address from the balcony of a government office building. The building was called the Casa Rosada ("Pink House"). A crowd had gathered below, and was chanting "Evita! Evita!"

LIFE EVENTS

1919
María Eva Duarte is born.

1926
Eva's father dies, leaving the family poor.

1935
Eva moves to Buenos Aires to become an actor.

1946
Eva's husband, Juan Perón, is elected president. Evita becomes First Lady.

1947
Evita Perón establishes programs to help the poor. She also fights for women's suffrage, which is granted.

1951
The Argentine people want Evita to run for vice president, but she cannot.

1952
Eva Perón dies of cancer.

A Place in History

On July 26, 1952, Eva Perón died of cancer in Buenos Aires. Hundreds of thousands of people lined the streets to pay their respects. In 1955, Eva's body was stolen by military leaders who did not want her memory to live on in Argentina. It was finally returned in 1974. Eva is now buried in the Duarte family tomb in Recoleta Cemetery in Buenos Aires.

In 1979, Eva was immortalized in a Broadway show, *Evita*, that chronicled her life. An audience favorite that later became a movie, it features the song "Don't Cry for Me, Argentina," sung from the balcony of the Casa Rosada. ◇

Molly Pitcher
(Mary Ludwig Hays McCauly)
Hero of the
American Revolution
(born 1754 • died 1832)

When Mary Ludwig was growing up in England's American colonies during the 1760s, she had no idea that they would soon become a new country called the United States of America. She could not have guessed that it would take a war for the colonies to win independence—or that, as "Molly Pitcher," she would become one of that war's most beloved heroes.

Growing Up

The Ludwigs were German immigrants who had moved to Great Britain's American colonies. Their daughter, Mary, was born on the family's dairy farm in Trenton, New Jersey, on October 13, 1754. Mary—or Molly, as she was called—spent her childhood carrying buckets of milk, herding cows out to pasture and back, and helping her family in other ways.

Molly Pitcher, the heroine of Monmouth, depicted in a lithograph by Nathaniel Currier

> **"While in the act of reaching for a cartridge, a cannon shot from the enemy passed directly between her legs without doing any other damage than carrying away all the lower part of her petticoat."**
>
> —Joseph Plumb Martin, a soldier from Connecticut

As Molly was growing up, many colonists were unhappy about British rule; especially about taxes. The 1764 Sugar Act raised taxes on products that colonists shipped to and from Great Britain. The 1765 Stamp Act required colonists to pay taxes on newspapers, legal documents, and other business papers. As the colonists grew angrier, they began to talk about going to war to win independence from Great Britain.

While Molly was still in her teens, she moved to Carlisle, Pennsylvania. There she worked as a servant to a doctor. Later, she met a barber named William Hays, and the two of them married.

Molly Goes to War

In April 1775, war broke out between Britain and the American colonies. The first battles were fought in Massachusetts, but the American Revolution soon spread to the other colonies.

Molly's husband joined the colonial army in 1777. Like many soldiers' wives of that time, Molly Hays followed the army as it marched. The women cooked, cleaned, and took care of sick or injured men.

On June 28, 1778, the American and British armies met at Monmouth, New Jersey. There, on a day that one report called "one of the hottest days ever," the two armies fought the Battle of Monmouth.

The soldiers suffered greatly in the terrible heat. Along with those who fell from wounds suffered in the battle, many men passed out from the high temperature. One of these men was Molly's husband. He was in charge of firing a cannon, but fainted in the hot sun.

When Molly saw how the American soldiers were suffering, she knew she had to help. The strength she had gained as a girl lugging buckets of milk around the dairy farm served her well that day. She carried buckets of water onto the battlefield and ladled out drinks to the thirsty soldiers. Grateful troops called her "Molly Pitcher" as she refilled her buckets at a nearby stream and went back to the battlefield time and time again. According to some stories, she even took over for her fallen husband, helping to load and fire his cannon.

Molly Pitcher's name was not forgotten after the battle. The story of her compassionate efforts was retold many times. It may even have become mixed up with stories of Margaret Corbin, another woman who followed her husband to war. When Corbin's husband was killed during the 1776 attack on Fort Washington, New York, she kept firing his cannon until she was wounded.

A Place in History

Whether or not she ever fired a shot, Molly Pitcher became known as a hero of the Battle of Monmouth. Some years after the war, William Hays died and Molly married George McCauley.

In 1822, Pennsylvania awarded Mary McCauley a

TOPICAL TIDBIT

Margaret Corbin

Margaret Cochran Corbin was the first woman to receive a pension (money for retirement) from the U.S. government as a disabled soldier. She relieved her slain husband at the cannon at the battle at Fort Washington on November 16, 1776. The British fire was murderous and Corbin suffered serious injury. Eventually, the British captured the fort, but the wounded were freed. Corbin never completely recovered from her wounds. She died in 1800. Today, she is buried near the site of the battle in Fort Tryon Park in New York City.

pension of $40 a year for wartime bravery.

Molly Pitcher died on January 22, 1832. She was 77 years old. A cannon and a sculpture were placed at her grave in Carlisle, Pennsylvania, to honor her. A monument to Molly Pitcher also stands at the battle site in Monmouth, New Jersey. ◇

LIFE EVENTS

1754
Mary Ludwig, called Molly, is born in Trenton, New Jersey.

1777
William Hays, Molly's husband, volunteers for the colonial army.

1778
At the Battle of Monmouth, Molly earns the nickname Molly Pitcher.

1822
The state of Pennsylvania awards her a pension of $40 a year.

1832
Molly Pitcher dies in Carlisle, Pennsylvania.

Pocahontas
Native American Princess
(born about 1595 • died 1617)

For some historical figures, it can be difficult to separate fact from fiction. Such is the case with Pocahontas. She was a Native American princess who met some of the first British settlers in America. Whether she was eager to help the colonists or forced to help them is debated. But this much is clear: As a young woman, Pocahontas influenced peaceful relations between Native Americans and British settlers.

"Playful One"

Originally named Matoaka, Pocahontas was born around 1595 near present-day Jamestown, Virginia. She was the daughter of Chief Wahunsonacock (also called Powhatan), who ruled more than 30 tribes in the area. The tribes were collectively called the Powhatan, sharing the chief's name.

Matoaka was an energetic and spirited child. She was a friendly girl and soon earned the nickname *Pocahontas*, meaning "Playful One" or "Little Plaything."

This engraving of Pocahontas appeared in John Smith's
The Generall Historie of Virginia, 1624.

The Powhatan lived in houses covered with mats of reeds or bark. Men and women worked together to make sure that their villages had enough food and supplies to survive, especially through the hard winters.

Men were hunters and warriors, protecting their villages from enemy groups who wanted to fight for food or land. Women tended crops, such as beans, squash, and corn. Although the Powhatan traded with other groups for food and supplies, their survival was based on how well they could provide for themselves.

The British Arrive

In 1607, Pocahontas and the Powhatan people faced a new threat to their survival—the arrival of British settlers. The British created the colony of Jamestown, named after their king. They wanted to make new lives for themselves, and many of them hoped to use the area's natural resources to make money.

The Powhatan and British ways of life were very different, so fighting sometimes broke out between the two groups. They did, however, try to maintain peace. When

"She is the instrument to preserve this colony from death, famine, and other instruments."

—John Smith on Pocahontas, 1616

the colonists ran out of supplies, they traded with the Powhatan for corn.

Still, each group was suspicious of the other. In December 1607, John Smith, a British captain, was captured by the Powhatan, who were going to kill him. According to legend, Pocahontas—then 12 years old—stepped in and begged her father to spare his life, which he did. However, some historians doubt that this really happened. Smith did not write about it until later in his life.

Living With the British

Pocahontas often visited Jamestown and was friendly with the colonists. After John Smith left the colony in 1609 to return to England, tensions between the groups increased. In 1613, Pocahontas was captured and held hostage by Captain Samuel Argall. The captain wanted to restore peace. He said that he would let the

TOPICAL TIDBIT

Separating Fact From Fiction

Moviemakers often change historical events if they think it will make a better story. In the 1995 Disney movie *Pocahontas*, the Powhatan princess is an adult when she saves John Smith. The movie shows her falling in love with Smith, not John Rolfe. Many people said that the true story of Pocahontas should have been filmed instead.

princess go in exchange for colonists being held by the Powhatan. Pocahontas was a prisoner for nearly a year. During that time, she became a Christian and took the name Rebecca.

While living with the British, Pocahontas met colonist John Rolfe, a tobacco farmer. They married on April 5, 1614. About a year later, they had a son, named Thomas. The union of the Powhatan princess and a British colonist helped restore peace.

In 1616, the Rolfes went to London, England, for a visit. Pocahontas was treated with respect and curiosity. Few British people had ever seen a Native American. She even met King James I.

A Life Cut Short

The Rolfes left England in March 1617 to head back to Virginia. But they returned

LIFE EVENTS

1595?
Matoaka is born to Chief Powhatan.

1607
British settlers arrive.

1613
Matoaka, now known as Pocahontas, is captured by the British.

1615
Pocahontas gives birth to Thomas, her son with her English husband, John Rolfe.

1616
The Rolfe family travels to London, where Pocahontas catches a life-threatening disease.

1617
Pocahontas dies.

1622
John Rolfe is killed in a clash with Indians.

1640
Thomas Rolfe, now an adult, returns to the colonies from England.

immediately to shore because Pocahontas suddenly became very sick.

She died soon afterward and was buried in Kent, England. She was 21. The cause of death was possibly smallpox, tuberculosis, or pneumonia. At that time, many Native Americans died from diseases common in Europe but not in North America. Their bodies had not yet developed the ability to fight off such diseases. After Pocahontas's death and the death of her father, war broke out between the colonists and the Powhatan. In 1622, John Rolfe was killed.

Even if the legends that surround Pocahontas are untrue, she remains known as a compassionate figure in American history. She worked to maintain peace and friendship at a time when tensions between two very different peoples were likely to erupt into war. ◇

Ernie Pyle
War Correspondent
(born 1900 • died 1945)

For many Americans, World War II was hard to understand. Then Ernie Pyle traveled to Europe's war-torn cities and began writing about the people he met and the things he saw. His simple, down-to-earth writing style gave Americans a clearer idea of what they were fighting for.

A Restless Young Man

Ernest Taylor Pyle was born on August 3, 1900, in the family home in Dana, Indiana. His parents were farmers, but young Ernie never liked living and working on the farm. Instead, he dreamed of far-away places where life was more exciting.

In 1919, he enrolled at Indiana University. He soon discovered that he had a natural talent for writing. By his second year, Ernie Pyle was writing for the college newspaper. He realized that journalists didn't just report the news: They could also enlighten and inspire people through their writing.

In 1923, Pyle quit school for a job as a reporter for a newspaper in La Porte, Indiana. Just a few months

Ernie Pyle worked on the front lines, reporting on the everyday lives of the troops there.

later, he moved on to a better job with the *Washington Daily News* in Washington, D.C. Pyle worked a number of jobs at the *News*, including reporting, editing copy, and writing a daily aviation column.

In 1935, Pyle became a roving reporter for the *News*. This job was perfect for his restless spirit. It allowed him to make his own schedule, travel to different places, talk with unusual and interesting people, and express his feelings in print. Within a year, Pyle had traveled thousands of miles and visited every state.

> **"There was nothing macho about the war at all. We were a bunch of scared kids who had a job to do."**
> —Ernie Pyle

His columns were published in about 200 different newspapers around the country.

The World at War

By 1940, Europe was being torn apart by World War II. In November, Pyle moved to London to write about life during wartime. At the time, London and other parts of England were being heavily bombed by Germany. Pyle was deeply affected by the bombings. He wrote moving columns describing his experience. By the time he returned to Washington in March 1941, he had become one of the most popular newspaper columnists in America.

In November 1942, Pyle and a number of other journalists joined U.S. troops in Algeria. Unlike the other reporters, Pyle didn't stay in the officers' quarters and report on military strategy. He stayed with the soldiers on the front lines and wrote about their everyday lives—how they washed their dishes with sand, what kind of food they ate, what it was like to see a friend killed in battle. His columns were full of details about these ordinary young men he called "the guys that wars can't be won without." He gave readers a compassionate look at what it was like to be a soldier. In turn, the soldiers treated Pyle like a beloved buddy. His columns made the soldiers feel that their sacrifices were appreciated by the folks back home.

TOPICAL TIDBIT

Bill Mauldin

Bill Mauldin was another newspaperman beloved by the men who fought World War II—but Mauldin's work was cartooning. Beginning in 1943 in Sicily, he drew cartoons for the U.S. Army newspaper, *Stars and Stripes*, that showed how the soldiers at the front line really lived. "Fresh American troops flushed with victory . . ." said one caption—while the picture showed men who were tired and covered with mud. Many of Mauldin's cartoons featured two battle-weary characters named Willie and Joe, who grew popular with both the soldiers and the folks back home.

By 1943, Pyle was the most popular war correspondent in America. His columns appeared in hundreds of newspapers and were read by millions of people. The columns were also published as a book, called *Here Is Your War*. (Three other books of Pyle's writings were published as well: *Ernie Pyle in England*, *Brave Men*, and *Last Chapter*.)

Pyle didn't care about being famous, though. When he returned to America for a brief vacation in 1943, he couldn't wait to go back to Europe and rejoin the soldiers there.

A New Front

In 1944, Pyle received news that he had won a Pulitzer Prize for distinguished correspondence. Later that year, he wrote his last column from Europe. Then he headed to the other

LIFE EVENTS

1900
Ernest Taylor Pyle is born in Dana, Indiana.

1923
Pyle quits school to work full-time as a reporter.

1940
Pyle's reporting on the bombardment of England begins to make him the most popular columnist in America.

1942
Pyle joins U.S. troops in Algeria.

1944
Pyle wins the Pulitzer Prize for his war columns.

1945
The Story of G.I. Joe, a movie based on Pyle's writing, is released. Pyle is killed by Japanese gunfire on the island of Ie Shima.

side of the world to write about the soldiers who were fighting against Japan on islands in the Pacific Ocean.

While in the Pacific, Pyle wrote about the 77th Infantry Division's invasion of Okinawa on April 1, 1945. A few days later, he traveled to a Japanese island called Ie Shima to write about an invasion taking place there. On April 18, while he was driving down a road on the island, he was killed by machine-gun fire. He was 44 years old.

News of Ernie Pyle's death stunned America. President Harry S. Truman honored him as a man who "told the story of the American fighting man as American fighting men wanted it told."

Pyle was buried on Ie Shima, along with U.S. soldiers also killed on the island. Later, his body was moved to the National Memorial Cemetery of the Pacific, in Hawaii. A memorial marker stands at the place on Ie Shima where he was killed. "At this spot," says the plaque, "the 77th Infantry Division lost a buddy. Ernie Pyle. 18 April 1945." ◇

A. Philip Randolph

Labor Leader

(born 1889 • died 1979)

For many years, African Americans were not represented by labor unions. A. Philip Randolph changed that, and helped win fair and equal treatment for black workers all over America.

Racial Tensions

Asa Philip Randolph was born on April 15, 1889, in Crescent City, Florida. When he was two years old, his family moved to Jacksonville, Florida. Jacksonville was one of the most integrated cities in the South. This meant that black and whites lived in the same communities, rode the same streetcars, and shopped in the same stores. Blacks also were able to serve as city council members, judges, and in other positions of authority. However, things changed during the early 1900s. Segregation laws

A. Philip Randolph dedicated his life to seeking equal treatment for all workers.

erased many freedoms. Discrimination against African Americans grew.

The Randolph family was very poor. Despite their poverty, Asa's father, a minister, made sure that his children were proud and self-confident. He encouraged them to stand up to discrimination and to be leaders in helping others.

Education was also very important in the Randolph family. Asa and his older brother did well in school. But there wasn't enough money for them to go to college. Instead, Asa worked at a variety of jobs while he tried to decide what he wanted to do with his life.

Organizing Black Workers

In 1911, 22-year-old A. Philip Randolph moved to Harlem, a black community in New York City. He worked at a number of jobs while attending City College at night. In 1917, Randolph and a friend, Chandler Owen, started a magazine called *The Messenger*. It called for more opportunities for blacks in industry. In those days, that was a radical position to take. The government said that *The Messenger* was "the most dangerous of all the Negro publications," because it called for racial equality at home.

Randolph wanted to see blacks gain political power. He realized that this could happen only if black workers belonged to labor unions. Labor unions are groups formed by workers to protect their rights. However, most labor unions refused to admit black members.

In 1925, Randolph was asked to advise a group of railroad porters about how to start their own union. Railroad porters were men who carried luggage and performed other services for passengers. They all worked for the Pullman Company, which operated the sleeping cars used on long-distance trains. The porters thought that they were underpaid and badly treated. They were so excited by Randolph's speech that they asked him to lead their new union. He agreed.

By the end of 1926, the Brotherhood of Sleeping Car Porters had thousands of members all over the country. It represented more than half of all the porters who worked for the Pullman Company.

The Pullman Company was very angry about the new union. Union leaders were threatened and beaten, and porters who were seen with union organizers were fired. The Pullman Company also sent letters to the black community criticizing Randolph. They said that he was trying to deny jobs to black workers. Randolph himself had so little money that he had only one suit to wear, and he and his wife relied on their friends to bring them food.

Despite these hardships, the Brotherhood grew stronger. In 1937, the union won its first major contract with the Pullman Company. Randolph was recognized as one of the most important leaders in the black community and in the U.S. labor movement.

> "Let the nation and the world know the meaning of our numbers. We are the advance guard of a massive moral revolution for jobs and freedom."
>
> —A. Philip Randolph, at the March on Washington, 1963

More Victories

Randolph's victories with the Brotherhood were only the beginning of his fight for equality. During the 1940s, Randolph called for the government to pass legislation that did away with discrimination. His efforts led to the passage of presidential orders banning discrimination in defense industries and federal bureaus (1941) and ending segregation in the military (1948).

Later, Randolph served as vice president of America's largest union, the AFL-CIO, from 1955 to

1977. He also served as the first president of the Negro American Labor Council, from 1960 to 1966.

Randolph's most dramatic accomplishment, however, was directing the March on Washington for Jobs and Freedom. On August 28, 1963, nearly 250,000 people gathered on the Mall in the nation's capital to demonstrate for equal rights for blacks. Millions of Americans, watching the march on TV, saw the power and purpose of the civil-rights movement for the first time. No one would forget the "I Have a Dream" speech that Martin Luther King Jr. made that day. In it, he described his dream for America: That one day, people of all races would live peacefully together, hand in hand.

TOPICAL TIDBIT

The March That Finally Came to Pass

A. Philip Randolph had dreamed for years of a march on Washington. He originally called one for July 1, 1941, to demand racial equality in the nation's defense plants. "We loyal Negro American citizens demand the right to work and fight for our country," he said. President Franklin D. Roosevelt was worried that the U.S. might soon have to join World War II, already being fought in Europe. He asked Randolph to call off the march. When he refused, Roosevelt issued an executive order banning discrimination in defense plants. With that victory won, Randolph tackled other problems—and put off his march for another 22 years.

It remains one of the most important speeches in U.S history. Randolph's efforts in organizing the march helped make that speech possible.

Randolph's health began to fail during the 1960s. He resigned as president of the Brotherhood in 1968, after 43 years in office. A. Philip Randolph died in New York City on May 16, 1979, at the age of 90. His life had set an example of how dignity, courage, and compassion could triumph over ignorance and injustice. ◇

LIFE EVENTS

1889
Asa Philip Randolph is born in Crescent City, Florida.

1925
Randolph is founding president of the Brotherhood of Sleeping Car Porters.

1937
The union wins its first major contract with the Pullman Company.

1941
Randolph's actions lead to the federal ban of job discrimination in defense industries.

1963
Randolph directs the March on Washington for Jobs and Freedom.

1968
Randolph retires from the Brotherhood. He dies in 1979 at age 90.

Eleanor Roosevelt
Social Reformer, First Lady
(born 1884 • died 1962)

Eleanor Roosevelt was an important social reformer, as well as First Lady. She was devoted to many social causes, including ending poverty and addressing race and women's issues. In many ways, she was ahead of her time in the issues she tackled. She left an excellent example of leadership and compassion for future generations to follow.

Overcoming Shyness

Anna Eleanor Roosevelt was born on October 11, 1884, in New York City. She was the niece of Theodore Roosevelt, who was president of the United States from 1901 to 1909. During Eleanor's childhood, both of her parents died and she was sent to live with her grandmother. Unlike her beautiful mother, Eleanor was a plain-looking girl. She was very shy and lacked self-confidence.

Eleanor Roosevelt, photographed in July 1933

At 15, she was sent to a girls' school in England. There, Eleanor slowly overcame her shyness and gained confidence. The school's principal thought that Eleanor had strong leadership qualities.

Three years later, Eleanor returned to New York. Interested in social issues, she taught dance and exercise classes to people living in the city's poor neighborhoods. In 1903, she was engaged to Franklin D. Roosevelt (known as FDR), a distant cousin. They married on March 17, 1905.

> "I could not, at any age, be content to take my place by the fireside and simply look on. Life was meant to be lived, and curiosity must be kept alive. One must never, for whatever reason, turn his back on life."
>
> —Eleanor Roosevelt

Life With FDR

Franklin Roosevelt devoted his career to public service. During the first 11 years of marriage, Franklin and Eleanor had five children. They also got involved in politics. In 1910, Franklin became a senator from New York. Eleanor assisted her husband with his political duties. In 1918, during World War I, Eleanor volunteered with the American Red Cross and in Navy hospitals.

In 1921, Franklin came down with polio, a disease that affected his legs, making it difficult to walk. Encouraged by Eleanor, he continued in politics despite his disability. She often traveled around the country to see what was happening in different communities across the states. Then she reported her findings to her husband. In 1928, he was elected governor of New York.

Eleanor pursued her own interests, too. She and some of her friends built a rustic cottage north of New York City. In 1926, they co-founded Val-kill Industries, a furniture factory, there. It was designed to give jobs to local youths and to keep the local economy strong.

Becoming the First Lady

In 1933, Franklin D. Roosevelt became the 32nd president of the United States. At that time, many politicians' wives stayed in the background. Not Eleanor. She took up women's and civil-rights causes. She openly disagreed with her husband when she believed that she should speak out. Unlike other politicians, Franklin truly respected his wife and her ideas. Even as president, he frequently asked Eleanor's advice.

Franklin was reelected three times. During his 12 years in office, he and Eleanor saw the nation through the Great Depression and World War II. During the Depression, Franklin established work programs to keep people employed, and Eleanor made sure that women and minorities were included in those programs. During the war, the Roosevelts built morale for the American public and put women to work in jobs left by men who had been sent to the front lines.

Eleanor began holding press conferences at the White House. She was the first First Lady to do so. When she started inviting only female journalists to the press conferences, she forced many of the nation's top newspapers to hire female reporters for the first time.

A Continuing Influence

Eleanor Roosevelt continued to influence history. She wrote her own newspaper column, called "My Day," from 1935 until her death. She fought to

TOPICAL TIDBIT

The Four-term President

Franklin Delano Roosevelt was the only U.S. president to be elected four times. In 1951, the 22nd Amendment to the Constitution became law. It states that no person can be elected to the U.S. presidency more than two times.

end racial segregation laws, which created separate areas (such as beaches, parks, and schools) for whites and blacks. At a meeting in Alabama in 1939, she caused a stir by sitting in the black section of seats instead of the whites-only section. With her help, segregation ended in the Army Nurse Corps in 1945.

When Franklin died in 1945, Eleanor thought that her political career was over. However, the new president, Harry S. Truman, appointed her as U.S. delegate to the United Nations (UN). She led the UN's Human Rights Commission in creating the Declaration of Human Rights, which was completed in 1948. In 1961, President John F. Kennedy appointed her as the first chairperson of the President's Commission on the Status of Women.

LIFE EVENTS

1884
Anna Eleanor Roosevelt is born in New York City.

1905
Eleanor marries Franklin Delano Roosevelt.

1933
Franklin becomes president.

1945
President Harry S. Truman appoints Eleanor Roosevelt as a delegate to the United Nations.

1948
Eleanor Roosevelt is a major contributor to the UN's Universal Declaration of Human Rights.

1958
On My Own, Roosevelt's autobiography, is published. She dies in 1962.

Eleanor Roosevelt died on November 7, 1962, in New York City. She had always shown great compassion to others, and was respected and admired by people worldwide.

Many historians believe that Eleanor Roosevelt achieved more than any other First Lady. She furthered women's rights, human rights, and civil rights in the U.S. and abroad. She was inducted into the National Women's Hall of Fame, and named one of the most influential people of the 20th century by *Time* magazine. People can visit her cottage home, now called the Eleanor Roosevelt National Historic Site, in Hyde Park, New York. ◇

Mother Teresa
Catholic Nun
(born 1910 • died 1997)

Mother Teresa blesses orphaned children at Children's Home in Calcutta, India, in October 1979.

Mother Teresa was only a teenager when she devoted her life to God and became a Catholic nun. She felt destined to work with the homeless and the sick in India. She believed that all people need to feel love, dignity, and compassion, and she opened centers to help those who were dying. She lived a simple life, with few possessions and without luxuries.

Becoming a Nun

Agnes Gonxha Bojaxhiu was born on August 27, 1910, in what is now Skopje, Macedonia. Her parents were Albanian. Agnes's father was murdered when Agnes was just seven years old. At 18, Agnes went to Ireland to become a nun with the Sisters of Our Lady of Loreto. She worked in Ireland, then in India, as she studied to become a nun.

> "Let us make one point, that we meet each other with a smile, when it is difficult to smile."
>
> —Mother Teresa

Often, when people devote their lives to God, they are said to "hear a calling." This means that they believe God has called on them to do his work on Earth, by helping the poor and sick, ministering to others about religion, or helping those in great need. Nuns usually live with few material possessions.

In 1937, when Agnes Bojaxhiu was 27 years old, she took the vow to serve God and became a nun. She took the name Teresa, after St. Teresa of Lisieux, the patron saint of foreign missionaries.

Teresa of Calcutta

Sister Teresa served as a teacher at St. Mary's High School in Calcutta, India. In 1944, she became principal. Then Sister Teresa became sick with tuberculosis. She had to take time out to rest and recover. During this time, she received a second calling from God. She believed that she was being called to work with the homeless, sick, and dying people among the poor in India.

In Calcutta, Sister Teresa saw many people living a life of poverty—some in the slums of the city, others on the street. When she found a dying

TOPICAL TIDBIT

The Little Flower

St. Teresa of Lisieux (1873-1897), Mother Teresa's namesake, was known as the "little flower." She wrote a short autobiography that many people have turned to in times of need. People have said that they were cured of their ailments after reading her book. Some people believe that seeing a rose—in a garden, in a picture, anywhere—is a sign that St. Teresa is working on their behalf.

woman surrounded by rats in the street, Sister Teresa knew that it was her destiny to live and work with the poor. The local hospital did not want to help the woman because she had no money. Sister Teresa took some medical courses so that she could provide health care to the poor. Others soon joined her in this work.

In 1948, Sister Teresa began a new order of nuns, called the Missionaries of Charity. As the head of the order, Sister Teresa came to be called Mother Teresa. In 1952, the order opened a center to help poor people who were near death.

Mother Teresa's Ministry Expands

In addition to the nuns and priests who worked at the center, many volunteers devoted time and money to the cause. In time, the Missionaries of Charity branched out to do its work in hundreds of centers worldwide, including centers for people with AIDS in New York and San Francisco.

The centers also include homes for disabled, orphaned, or adandoned children, as well as for lepers (people with leprosy, a life-threatening disease that causes deformities and paralysis). Mother Teresa sacrificed personal comfort to devote more money to her work. She believed that people should be able to live and die with dignity.

Spreading Peace

Mother Teresa served as an example of how much one person can accomplish. During her lifetime, she sought world peace and an end to human suffering. Among the awards she received were the Pope John XXIII Peace Prize (1971) and the Nobel Peace Prize (1979). True to her beliefs, Mother Teresa asked that the traditional Nobel Prize dinner not be held in her honor. She asked that the money for the dinner be devoted to her charity work instead, so that hundreds of people could be fed for an entire year.

Mother Teresa died of a heart attack on September 5, 1997. She was 87 years old. ◇

LIFE EVENTS

1910
Agnes Gonxha Bojaxhiu is born in what is now Skopje, Macedonia.

1928
Bojaxhiu travels to India to teach at a convent school.

1937
Bojaxhiu takes her vows as a nun, becoming Sister Teresa.

1948
Sister Teresa leaves the convent to work independently in the slums of India, becoming Mother Teresa.

1979
Mother Teresa is awarded the Nobel Peace Prize.

1997
Mother Teresa dies.

Roger Williams
A Home for Freedom
(born 1603? • died 1683)

Roger Williams and followers left Massachusetts to found the colony of Providence in 1636.

Today, Americans take it for granted that we can practice whatever religion we want. We owe much of that freedom to a brave man named Roger Williams. He was the first religious leader in America to declare that everyone should be free to worship as he or she chooses.

London Born and Bred

No one is sure exactly when Roger Williams was born, but historians generally agree that it was around 1603. He was born in London, England, the center of Great Britain's government and cultural life.

Roger's father was a merchant and tailor. The Williams family lived in a comfortable home near the Thames River. Like most other boys of his economic class, young Roger went to school. He also spent a great deal of time studying the Bible.

In 1621, Roger Williams met a judge named Sir Edward Coke. Coke was impressed with the young man and hired Williams as his secretary. He also arranged for Williams to attend one of England's best schools. In 1627, Williams graduated from Cambridge University. Two years later, he was ordained as a minister.

> "I acknowledge that to molest any person, Jew or Gentile, for . . . practicing worship merely religious or spiritual, it is to persecute him."
>
> —Roger Williams

Roger Williams had strong religious beliefs that went against the teachings of the Church of England. After he found himself in trouble with church leaders, he decided to sail for Britain's American colonies on December 1, 1630.

Trouble in Massachusetts

Williams arrived in the Massachusetts colony. He was soon offered the position of minister to the Boston congregation. However, he turned it down because he thought that the Boston church was too similar to the Church of England. Instead, he moved to Plymouth, Massachusetts, where he farmed and preached. Later, he became a minister in Salem, Massachusetts, even though the colony's Puritan leaders opposed his appointment.

The more Williams spoke out for freedom of religion, the more the leaders disliked him. He also made enemies when he said that there should be a complete separation of church and government. This meant that the government could not punish somebody who broke a church law. Only the church should handle such matters, Williams said.

Another belief that got him in trouble was that Native Americans should be treated fairly. While in Plymouth, Williams had become friends with the Narragansett Indians. In Salem, he declared that no one in Massachusetts had the right to take any land unless they bought it fairly from the Native Americans, because the Native Americans had been here and lived on the land first.

By October 1635, the Massachusetts colony's leaders had had enough of Roger Williams and his "dangerous" ideas. In a trial in the Massachusetts General Court, Williams was called an "offensive rebel" and an "evil-worker." He was exiled (sent away) from the colony. However, since winter was coming and Williams's wife was expecting a baby, he was allowed to stay until the spring, as long as he stopped preaching.

But Williams did not stop preaching. Instead, he gathered a group of followers and planned to form a new colony. When Massachusetts leaders found out what Williams was planning, they sent troops to arrest him. However, Williams had been warned of the plan. He and his followers escaped into the wilderness.

A New Colony

The Native Americans cared for Williams and his friends and helped them survive the winter. In the spring of 1636, Williams founded the settlement of Providence, on land that he purchased from the Narragansett Indians. Providence's government was based on total religious freedom and

LIFE EVENTS

About 1603
Roger Williams is born in London, England.

1631
Williams arrives in Boston, in the Massachusetts Bay Colony.

1635
Williams is banished from Massachusetts for preaching ideas opposed by church leaders.

1636
Williams founds the settlement of Providence in what is now Rhode Island.

1654
Williams becomes president of the colony of Rhode Island. He serves three terms.

1683
Roger Williams dies.

the separation of church and state. Every household had a voice in the government and received an equal share of the land. Soon the colony became a welcoming home for people who didn't agree with the strict rules of other colonies.

Williams also continued working with the Narragansett Indians. He negotiated peace treaties between the Narragansett and other tribes. He also helped settle or avoid conflicts between Native Americans and English settlers.

In 1643, Williams traveled to England to obtain a charter (written legal document) from the king. The charter made the settlements of Rhode Island and "the Providence Plantations in Narragansett Bay"

TOPICAL TIDBIT

The Narragansett Indians

Roger Williams and his followers owed their survival in the wilderness to the peaceful Narrangansett Indians of present-day Rhode Island. In time, however, new white settlers claimed more and more territory from the New England Indian tribes. In 1675, warriors of the Wampanoag tribe fought back. Other tribes, including the Narragansett, joined them in a series of bloody battles that became known as King Philip's War. (King Philip was the English name for Metacom, the Wampanoag chief.) The war was a tragedy for the Indians. When they lost, they split up and abandoned the area to the settlers.

into a new colony. In 1654, he was elected to the first of three terms as the first president of the colony.

Roger Williams remained active in his colony's political life until his death early in 1683. He lived his life as an honest, compassionate, open-minded man who respected everyone, no matter what they believed in or whether they were European or Native American. His ideas helped shape the ideals and laws of the United States, a nation born nearly a century after his death. ◇

Glossary and Pronunciation Guide

amendment *(uh-MEND-munt)* a change in wording or meaning in a law or the Constitution; *p. 16*

amputate *(AM-pyoo-tayt)* to surgically remove a part of the body; *p. 14*

communist *(KAHM-yuh-nist)* following a system in which the government owns or controls all economic production, goods, and services; *p. 29*

concentration camps *(kahn-sun-TRAY-shun KAMPS)* places where people are kept against their will under harsh conditions; *p.42*

conspiring *(kun-SPY-ring)* agreeing with others secretly to do something; *p. 61*

correspondent *(kor-uh-SPAHN-dunt)* a person who contributes news to a newspaper or newscast, often from a faraway place; *p. 93*

depression *(dih PREH-shun)* in economic terms, a period of widespread low economic activity and rising unemployment; *p. 17*; in medical terms, an illness marked by sadness, inactivity, and loss of a sense of one's own worth; *p. 23*

discrimination *(dis-krih-muh-NAY-shun)* different or unequal treatment; *p. 101*

Holocaust *(HAH-luh-kost)* the mass killing of European Jews by the Nazis during World War II; *p. 45*

humanitarian *(hyoo-man-uh-TER-ee-un)* a person who works for the health and happiness of other people; *p. 14*

illustrious *(ih-LUS-tree-us)* outstanding; *p. 77*

migration *(my-GRAY-shun)* movement from one place to another; *p. 56*

morale *(muh-RAL)* the feeling a group has about its common purpose; *p. 110*

negotiated *(nih-GOH-shee-ay-ted)* discussed with another person or group to come to an agreement; *p. 123*

plantation *(plan-TAY-shun)* a large farm or other land area worked by laborers; *p. 35*

plight *(PLYTE)* a difficult situation; *p. 20*

radical *(RA-dih-kul)* against popular opinion to an extreme degree; *p. 101*

reform *(rih-FORM)* to make better; *p. 7*

refugees *(REF-yoo-jeez)* people who flee to another place, seeking safety; *p. 29*

registering *(REH-juh-stur-ing)* officially signing up, especially as a voter or student; *p. 19*

roving *(ROHV-ing)* wandering; *p. 95*

rustic *(RUS-tik)* of the country; rural; *p. 49*

strike *(STRYKE)* when a group of workers stops working to force an employer to meet demands; *p. 20*

strikebreakers *(STRYKE-bray-kurz)* people hired to replace striking workers; *p. 60*

textile *(TEK-styl)* woven or knit cloth; *p. 60*